Live Action

Running

Andrew Langley

Chrysalis Education

Distributed in the United States by
Smart Apple Media
2140 Howard Drive West
North Mankato, Minnesota 56003

Library of Congress Control Number: 2003116866

ISBN 1-59389-148-2

Editorial Manager: Joyce Bentley
Project Editors: Lionel Bender and Clare Lewis
Designer: Ben White
Production: Kim Richardson
Picture Researcher: Cathy Stastny

Produced by Bender Richardson White, U.K.

Printed in China

10 9 8 7 6 5 4 3 2 1

Words in **bold** can be found in Words to remember on page 31.

Picture credits
Corbic: 10 (Paul Barton), 15 (Jeff Vanuga), 17 (Galen Rowell), 19, 25 (Gallo Images). Natural
History Photo Agency: 13 (Manfred Danegger), 27 (J. and A. Scott). Digital Vision: 1, 4, 6, 9.
Rex Features Ltd: 7 (Darren Banks), 8 (Sipa), 11 (Jim Pickerell), 12 (John Powell), 18 (Sunset),
20 (Henry T. Kaiser), 21 (Richard Austin), 22 (Sipa), 23 (Lehtikuva), 29 (Fotos International).
Steve Gorton: 14, 16, 24, 26, 28. Cover: Corbis/Larry Williams (main image), Steve
Gorton (back, front inset far right), Digital Vision (front insets far left, centre left),
Ecoscene/Sally Morgan (front inset centre right). Illustration page 5: Jim Robins.

Contents

Moving with muscles

People and animals run when they want to get somewhere quickly. Running is faster than walking. When you run, you jump forward from one foot to the other.

To run, you bend your legs. When you walk, you keep your legs straight.

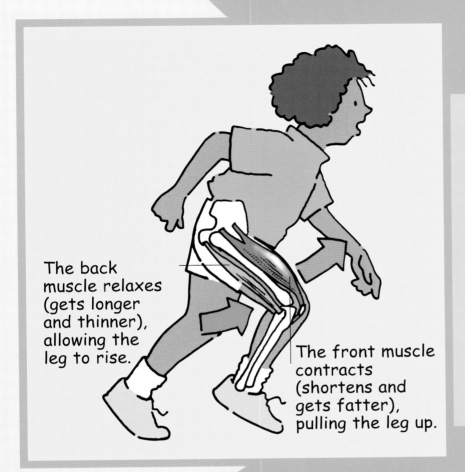

The back muscle relaxes (gets longer and thinner), allowing the leg to rise.

The front muscle contracts (shortens and gets fatter), pulling the leg up.

Muscles work in pairs. One muscle contracts while the other muscle relaxes. In this way, muscles move the bones in your skeleton forward and back to help you to run.

There are more than 600 different muscles in a human body, as well as more than 200 bones.

You use **muscles** to make you run. Muscles move the bones of your legs at the **joints**, such as your hips and knees.

Starting

Athletes get ready for a race by crouching down. To start, they rise up, push their feet hard against the ground, and run forward.

Athletes begin to run when the starter fires a pistol.

6

Lions get ready to chase their **prey** by crouching down with all four legs bent. They start to run by straightening their legs.

A lion must run very fast to catch antelopes or zebra, which can move swiftly away.

A lion pulls in its claws when it runs, so that they don't catch in the ground and slow it down.

Running fast

People run fast to win races, play games, catch a bus, or train, or just to have fun. Some animals run fast so that they can catch and eat their prey.

Sprinters train to make their leg muscles strong so that they can run quicker.

A sprinter can run at 23 miles an hour (37 km/h). An ostrich can go faster at 30 miles an hour (50 km/h).

An ostrich, with its long, slim legs, can run faster than any other bird.

Sprinting, or running fast, uses up a lot of **energy**. This energy comes from food. Our body turns the food we eat into energy for our muscles to work.

Jogging

If you run far at top speed, you use up your energy quickly. To keep running for a long distance, you need to run slowly or jog.

Jogging is running slowly. This family is jogging so they don't get tired too quickly.

A horse running slowly is called **trotting**. As it runs faster, we say it **canters**. At top speed, the horse **gallops**.

A horse can keep trotting at 9 miles an hour (14 km/h) for several hours.

Horses have big, thick muscles in the upper part of their legs and thin muscles in the lower part.

Running around

Running can be fun. In chasing games, you run fast and then slow, and then fast again —and never in a straight line!

Playing running games in the park is a fun way to keep fit and healthy.

Some animals like to play
running games, too. Baby
hares chase each other
round and round in circles.

Players run
around all the
time in team
sports such as
soccer, rugby,
and hockey.

Running around
helps young hares make
their muscles grow and
become strong.

Going uphill

Running up a hill is much harder than running on level ground. Your muscles must do more work to move your legs and push you up the hill.

This runner is taking part in a cross-country race. He runs up and down hills.

To run well uphill, lean forward a little, and take shorter strides.

Animals with four legs, such as dogs, can run up a hill very quickly. Their front legs keep them steady, while their stronger and longer back legs push them forward.

Wolves run in snow by springing along on their toes.

Going downhill

Running down a hill is also hard work.
Your leg muscles have to stop your knees
bending too much to slow you down.

Don't run downhill too fast—you could
lose your balance and fall.

Bighorn sheep run around on mountain slopes in North America.

Sheep put their front feet down first, then their back feet. This stops them falling over.

Running on four legs makes it easier to go down downhill. A sheep pushes its front feet into the ground to stop it falling.

Running together

In long races, athletes often run along together. No one wants to run ahead too fast and tire quickly. Nor does an athlete want to be left behind.

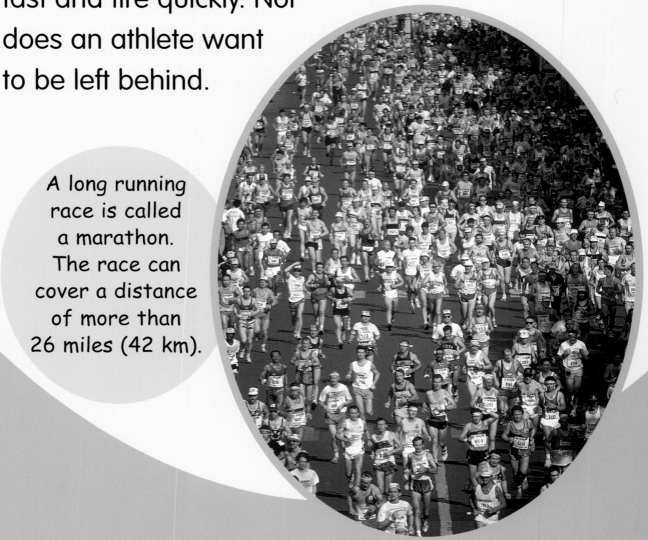

A long running race is called a marathon. The race can cover a distance of more than 26 miles (42 km).

Buffalo move about in large **herds** as they search for food. If they are attacked, they run away together as a group.

By running away together as a herd, the buffalo make it more difficult for a predator to catch them.

African buffalo are as big as cows but can run at speeds of 28 miles an hour (45 km/h).

Running in water

Running in shallow water at the beach is great fun. But your leg muscles have to work hard to lift your feet and push against the water.

The deeper the water, the harder it is to move and run in the water.

Some animals can actually run on top of the water. Swans run on the surface of lakes and ponds in order to take off.

Oystercatchers, plovers, and sandpipers are all birds known as waders. They can often be seen running in water along seashores.

Swans have broad, flat feet that act like paddles.

Going steady

Athletes do not want to waste energy when they run. So they learn to run the correct way, with even strides that are not too long.

Runners move their arms back and forth to help balance them.

Reindeer can run a long way without wasting energy. They can keep up a steady speed with their long legs.

Reindeer run across the wide, open areas of Canada, Norway, Sweden, Finland, and Russia.

Reindeer can run up to 20 miles (32 km) without tiring.

Carrying a load

Hikers can run with heavy **packs** on their backs. Carrying the extra weight uses up more energy.

Soldiers are trained to run with equipment weighing as much as 66 pounds (30 kg).

You need tough boots to cope with running across rough or boggy ground.

Chimpanzees run on all fours, using their long arms as front legs.

Chimpanzee mothers carry their young babies with them as they run along. Newborn babies cling to the fur on their mother's belly.

Running a race

People run races against each other to see who is the fastest. They get ready at the starting line and set off together.

The race winner is the first person to cross the finishing line.

Some animals, like zebra, live in herds. When a herd is alarmed, all the zebra start to run in the same direction. They race to escape a predator.

Zebra run across the grasslands of Africa. Animals with four legs run faster than those with two legs.

Some animals in the herd will be the leaders and run at the front while the others follow as if in a race.

Stopping

When you are running fast, it is hard to stop suddenly. Even when you have stopped, your body will go on using up energy.

After running, you will feel hot and out of breath until your temperature returns to normal.

To stop running, shorten your stride and put your legs firmly on the ground.

An animal with four legs finds it easier to stop quickly. It braces its legs, leans back, and skids to a halt.

The bigger the animal, the longer it will take to stop quickly.

Facts and figures

A sprinter can run as fast as 23 miles an hour (37 km/h). The fastest animal on land, the cheetah, can run as fast as 56 miles an hour (90 km/h).

In races, horses can reach a speed of about 38 miles an hour (60 km/h). Greyhound dogs can run up to 35 miles an hour (56 km/h).

Beetles can run at about 2 miles an hour (3 km/h). A snail's fastest speed is about 33 feet (10 m) an hour.

Footprints of a medium-sized dinosaur show it may have been able to run at speeds of up to 27 miles an hour (43 km/h).

Arvind Pandya ran backward across the whole of North America. The journey took him 107 days.

The oldest woman to run a marathon is Scotland's Jenny Wood-Allen. She completed the 2002 London Marathon in the U.K. at the age of 90.

Mexican Arturo Barrios has run further in one hour than anyone else. He covered 13 miles 400 yards (21.1 km) in France in 1991.

The quickest ever run up the Empire State Building in New York, U.S., was performed by Australian Paul Crake. He ran up the 1576 steps in 9 minutes 33 seconds.

Athlete   Someone who takes part in sports such as running.

Canter   The way a horse runs that is just slower than a gallop.

Energy   The power that lets us exercise and move our bodies.

Gallop   The way a horse runs at top speed so that at times all its feet are off the ground.

Herd   A large group of animals. The animals often run together as a group.

Joint   A part of the skeleton where two bones meet.

Muscle   A bundle of elastic-like fibers that can tighten or relax to move parts of our bodies.

Pack   A bag worn on the back for carrying such things as a tent or clothes.

Predator   An animal that attacks and eats other animals.

Prey   An animal that is hunted and caught for food.

Sprint   To run at top speed.

Stride   To move forward usually with long steps.

Trot   The way a horse runs that is faster than a walk but slower than a canter.

Index